Pies Aplenty

Produced by the staff of *Farm Wife News*

Edited by Annette Gohlke, Food Editor

Illustrations by Peggy Bjorkman

Production: Sally Radtke, Sue DesRochers

Assistant Editors: Ann Kaiser, Lynn Wahner

ISBN 0-89821-007-0
Reiman Publications, Inc.
P.O. Box 643
Milwaukee, Wisconsin 53201

SECOND PRINTING

From Our Kitchen

Dear Friends of <u>Farm</u> <u>Wife</u> <u>News</u>:

Here is the pie book you've been asking for . . . fresh from the recipe testing ovens of our <u>Farm</u> <u>Wife</u> <u>News</u> kitchen.

Actually, this is <u>your</u> book more than ours, for in it we have compiled the best of the hundreds of pie recipes sent to us by you and your cohorts—farm and ranch wives across America—who competed in our "Rural Recipe Roundup Pie Contest."

We received more recipes for this contest than any other we've ever run, and it's easy to understand why: Farmer husbands usually rate pies Number One on their dessert list.

We regard you rural cooks as some of our best friends—we feel we've really gotten to know you during these past few years, because so many of you take time to include a short note when you send us your recipes. They're like "letters from home".

So we're dedicating this book to you, our friends of <u>Farm</u> <u>Wife</u> <u>News</u>, with the hope that you enjoy each family-pleasing, husband-holding, guest-raving pie that you and other farm wives have been generous enough to share with each other.

Annette Gohlke

FWN Food Editor

Contents

Pie Crusts

GENERAL DIRECTIONS FOR MAKING PASTRY

To Mix

Chill all the ingredients. For the beginner, even the flour may be chilled. Measure the flour and salt into a chilled bowl. Work in the shortening or lard with a pastry blender, two knives or a fork until the particles are the size of small peas. Sprinkle with the ice water, 1 tablespoon at a time, stirring dough with a fork just until the particles are moistened and stick together to form a dough. Cover the dough and chill for 30 minutes or longer before rolling into a pie shell.

To Roll

Dust a board lightly with flour. A pastry cloth and a special stockinet cover for your rolling pin may be purchased. Lightly dust these with flour also before rolling the dough. Dough may also be rolled between two sheets of waxed paper. Divide a standard recipe for pastry in half and pat each piece of dough into a ball, flattening slightly. *Do not overhandle.* Place on prepared board and roll 1/4 to 1/8-inch thick. To roll, use short strokes from center to edges, turning the dough often to keep it round. If the dough splits at the edges, press together. Make the circle of dough 1 inch larger than the pie pan. If the dough sticks to the board as you are removing it to place into your pie pan, gently loosen it with a metal spatula. Fold in half for easier handling, place in the pie pan, unfold and loosely fit the crust to shape.

One Crust Pies

Loosely fit the crust into an ungreased pie pan. Shape to fit then trim dough 1/2 inch from edge of pan. Turn dough under and flute rim with your fingers or crimp with the tines of a fork. Fill and bake according to directions. If the recipe calls for a baked pie shell, follow the procedure above but prick the shell well to prevent dough from puffing. Bake in a hot oven 450° 10-12 minutes. Cool and fill.

Two Crust Pies

Divide the dough in two portions, one slightly larger than the other and use the larger portion for the bottom crust. Fit the crust loosely into the pie plate and fill. Trim crust leaving about 1/2 inch from edge. Moisten edge with cold water or a little egg white. Fold top crust in half, adjust over filling, open out to cover remaining half of pie and slash or prick top crust. Trim to meet bottom crust, fold under and press together with fingers; then flute or crimp together with a fork to seal. To flute, press edges with finger of the one hand and pinch the dough between thumb and forefinger of other hand.

Lattice top

Roll a circle of dough as for a crust and cut into 1/2-inch strips. Use a pastry wheel if you have one to make an attractive edge. Lay half the strips across the pie filling, 1 inch apart. Weave the cross strips over and under these, beginning at the center. Trim the ends of the strips, moisten edge of pastry with water and fold edge of bottom crust over strips. Press to seal.

PLAIN PASTRY ·

2 cups flour
1/2 teaspoon salt
1/2 cup shortening

1/4 cup butter
3 to 4 tablespoons cold water

Sift together flour and salt. Cut in shortening and butter until mixture resembles coarse meal. Add just enough water to make dough stick together. Form into ball. Chill about 15 to 20 minutes. Roll on floured canvas or board to 1/4 to 1/8-inch thick and line pie plate.

QUICK PASTRY ✓ 10 - 81

1/2 cup shortening
1/4 cup cold water
1-1/2 cup flour

1/2 teaspoon baking powder
1/2 teaspoon salt

Melt shortening, add water and mix with remaining ingredients to form a smooth dough. Chill before rolling on a floured board. Fit into a 9-inch pie pan.

NEVER-FAIL PIE CRUST

3 cups flour
1 teaspoon salt
1 cup lard or shortening

1 egg
1 teaspoon vinegar
5 tablespoons water or milk

In a large mixing bowl combine the flour, salt and lard and blend with a pastry blender until mixture resembles fine crumbs. In a small bowl beat the egg and add the vinegar and water. Pour over the flour and mix until dough forms. Let rest, or refrigerate until ready to roll out for pie.
—*Marjorie M. Letellier, Belvidere, South Dakota*

JIFFY PIE CRUSTS: *Plan a few hours devoted to preparing pie crusts for the freezer. Roll out and place the first crust in a metal pie tin, then pile consecutive crusts on top of each other, separating each with either a paper plate or double thickness waxed paper. Wrap and freeze. So good to have when you are short of time.* Mrs. Einar Tosse, Lidgerwood, North Dakota

PASTRY MIX

7 cups flour
4 teaspoons salt   2-1/3 cups lard (1 pound)

Combine flour and salt in large mixing bowl. Cut in lard with pastry blender until mixture resembles the texture of rice. Store in refrigerator and use as needed. 1-1/4 cup of mix yields 1 pie shell; 2 cups are needed for a double crust pie; 4 to 6 tablespoons of cold water are used for the 2 cup measure.

—Mrs. Hilbert Gerdes, Goodhue, Minnesota

CHOCOLATE PIE CRUST

1-1/4 cup flour
  1/3 cup sugar
  1/4 cup cocoa
  1/2 teaspoon salt

1/2 cup shortening
1/2 teaspoon vanilla
  2 to 3 tablespoons cold water

In a bowl combine the flour, sugar, cocoa and salt. Cut in the shortening until particles are the size of small peas. Sprinkle with 2 to 3 tablespoons cold water, add the vanilla and mix until dough forms. Roll the dough between 2 pieces of waxed paper to make a 11 or 12-inch circle. Fit pastry into a 9-inch pie pan, trim off excess dough and flute the edge. Place the dough trimmings on another small pan and bake the crust and trimmings in a 400° oven for 8 to 10 minutes. Do Not Overbake! Cool. Crumble the cooled trimmings and save for crumb topping on the pie.

—Mrs. Tom Blum, Morrill, Nebraska

GRAHAM CRACKER PIE SHELL

1 cup graham cracker crumbs
3 tablespoons light brown sugar

3 tablespoons butter, melted

Mix the ingredients and press into a 9-inch pie pan. Chill, freeze or bake before filling. To bake place in a 350° oven and bake for 10 minutes.

SODA CRACKER MERINGUE

3 egg whites
1/2 teaspoon baking powder
1 cup sugar

10 soda crackers, broken fine
1/2 cup pecans, chopped

Beat the egg whites and baking powder until stiff. Gradually add the sugar, beating well until whites become stiff and glossy. Fold in the crackers and pecans. Spread into a well greased 9-inch pie plate forming the meringue up the sides of the pan. Bake at 300° for 30 minutes. Cool.

—Mrs. Lois Beavers, Big Cabin, Oklahoma

MERINGUE PIE SHELL

2 egg whites
Dash salt
1/8 teaspoon cream of tartar

1/2 teaspoon vanilla
7 tablespoons sugar

Beat the egg whites until frothy then add the salt and cream of tartar. Beat until stiff but not dry. Add the vanilla and continue beating, adding 1 tablespoon of sugar at a time until egg whites are stiff and glossy. Spread on bottom and sides of a 9-inch greased pie plate. Bake at 375° for 1 hour. Turn off heat and leave in oven until cool.

—Roberta Moellenberg, Idalia, Colorado

SESAME SEED CRUST

1/4 cup sesame seeds, toasted
1 cup flour
1/2 teaspoon salt

1/3 cup oil
2 to 3 tablespoons milk

In a 325° oven toast the sesame seeds for 8 minutes. Add the seeds to the flour, salt, oil and milk. Form dough into ball and roll between waxed paper to fit an 8-inch pie pan. Prick and bake at 425° for 10 minutes or until golden brown.

—Mrs. Marlene Reed, Hales Corners, Wisconsin

Fruit Pies

APPLE-CRANBERRY "AUTUMN PIE"

1 9-inch pie shell, unbaked
3 cups apples, sliced
2 cups cranberries
3/4 cup sugar

1/4 cup flour
1 teaspoon cinnamon
1-1/2 teaspoon butter, melted

Combine all ingredients and put in pie shell. Top with pastry lattice strips. Bake at 350° for 1 hour or until apples are tender.

—*Mrs. R. Longnecker, West Plains, Missouri*

APPLE CIDER PIE

1 9-inch pie shell, unbaked
4 to 5 cups apples
1/2 cup raisins
1/2 teaspoon cinnamon
Dash of salt
1/4 teaspoon nutmeg
1/2 cup sugar

1 tablespoon lemon juice
1 cup apple cider
2 teaspoons lemon peel, grated
3 tablespoons butter
3 tablespoons flour
1 egg white
1 teaspoon water

Cinnamon Topping
1/4 cup pecans, chopped
1 tablespoon sugar

1/4 teaspoon cinnamon

In a saucepan melt the butter, blend in the flour and gradually add the cider, lemon juice and rind and cook until thick, stirring constantly. Beat together the egg white and water, just till combined. Brush part of this mixture over the bottom of the unbaked pie shell (this keeps the crust from becoming soggy). In a bowl combine the peeled, cored and sliced apples and raisins and mix together with the sugar and spices. Pile the mixture into the pie shell and pour the cider sauce over. Cover the pie with a lattice pastry top, brush with the egg white mixture and fill the spaces with the cinnamon topping. Bake at 350° for 40 to 50 minutes or until apples are tender and crust is nicely browned.

—Mrs. Wayne Faidley, Coats, Kansas

CINNAMON DANDY APPLE PIE

1 10-inch pie shell, unbaked
8 to 10 medium sized apples
3/4 cup sugar (adjust according
  to tartness of apples)

4 tablespoons flour
1/2 teaspoon salt
1/4-1/2 cup cinnamon candies

Wash, pare, core and slice apples. Combine sugar, flour, salt and cinnamon candies. Add to apples and mix. Put into crust and dot with butter. Cover with top crust. Bake at 450° for 15 minutes, then reduce heat to 350° for 25 to 30 minutes until pie is nicely browned and apples are tender.

—Mrs. Adolph Abbnehl, Prairie Farm, Wisconsin

MY APPLE PIE

1 9-inch pie shell, unbaked
1/2 cup orange juice
1/2 cup pineapple juice
1/4 cup brown sugar
1/2 cup white sugar
1/4 teaspoon salt

5 cups apples
2 tablespoons cornstarch
2 tablespoons lemon juice
2 tablespoons cherry juice
1/4 teaspoon nutmeg
1/2 teaspoon cinnamon

Combine orange juice, pineapple juice, sugars and salt. Bring to a boil and add sliced apples. Cook until tender (about 5 minutes). Remove apples from juice and add the combined cornstarch, lemon juice, cherry juice, cinnamon and nutmeg to liquid. Boil until thickened. Pour over cooked apples and put into the pie shell. Cover with the top crust, vent with slits, brush with water and sprinkle with sugar. Bake at 425° for 25 minutes. —Pat Waymire, Dayton, Ohio

DUTCH APPLE PIE

1 9-inch pie shell, unbaked
3 cups apples, sliced
1 cup sugar
3 tablespoons flour
1/2 teaspoon cinnamon
1 egg, beaten

1 cup light cream
1 teaspoon vanilla
1/2 cup nuts, chopped
1 tablespoon butter
1/2 cup sharp cheddar cheese, shredded

Place sliced apples in pastry shell. Mix sugar, flour and cinnamon. Combine egg, cream and vanilla. Add sugar mixture and mix well. Pour over apples. Sprinkle with nuts and dot with butter. Bake at 350° for 45 to 50 minutes or until apples are tender. Remove pie from oven and sprinkle with cheese. Serve warm.

—Mrs. Glen F. Bormann, LaMotte, Iowa

APPLE SHEET PIE

Crust

3 cups flour

1/4 cup sugar

1-1/2 teaspoon salt

1/2 cup butter

1/4 cup cooking oil

1 egg, unbeaten

1/4 cup cold water

Filling

2 cans apple pie filling

1/2 pound light caramels

1/2 cup evaporated milk

8 ounces cream cheese

1 egg, unbeaten

1/3 cup sugar

In a mixing bowl, sift together the flour, sugar and salt. Cut in the butter until mixture is fine. In a small bowl, blend the oil, egg and cold water until smooth and add to dry ingredients. Stir until mixture holds together. Roll out the dough on a pastry cloth or a large piece of tin foil to fit a jelly roll pan approximately 17 x 12 inches. Fill the crust with the apple pie filling. In a double boiler, melt the caramels and milk, stirring until smooth and blended. In a small bowl, mix the cream cheese, egg and sugar until smooth. Pour over the apple filling alternating strips of the caramel then the cheese mixture. Sprinkle the caramel strips with nuts. Bake at 375° for 35 minutes.

—Mrs. Francis Shaw, Mill Run, Pennsylvania

JOHNNY APPLESEED PIE

1 9-inch pie shell, unbaked

5 cups apples, sliced

1/3 cup sugar

1 teaspoon cinnamon

1/2 cup chocolate chips

1 cup biscuit mix

1/4 cup sugar

4 tablespoons butter

Mix first three ingredients together and turn into the pie shell. Sprinkle chocolate chips over the top. In a bowl, combine the biscuit mix and sugar and cut in the butter. Sprinkle over the pie. Bake at 400° for 45 minutes or until apples are tender.

—Mrs. Curtis Sykora, Windom, Minnesota

APPLE GINGERBREAD COBBLER

4 cups apples, sliced	2 tablespoons cooking oil
1/2 cup brown sugar, firmly packed	1 cup flour
1 tablespoon lemon juice	1/2 teaspoon baking soda
1/4 teaspoon cinnamon	1/2 teaspoon baking powder
1/4 cup sugar	1/2 teaspoon ginger
1 egg	1/4 teaspoon nutmeg
1/2 cup buttermilk	1/4 teaspoon salt
1/4 cup molasses	2 teaspoons cornstarch

Combine apples, brown sugar, 1 cup water, lemon juice and cinnamon. Cover and cook until apples are tender. Beat together the sugar, egg, buttermilk, molasses and oil. Combine the flour, baking soda, baking powder, spices and salt. Add to egg mixture and beat until smooth. Mix the cornstarch with 1 tablespoon cold water and stir into the apple mixture. Pour into a greased 1-1/2 quart casserole. Spoon the gingerbread mixture on top of the apples. Bake at 350⁰ for 30 minutes.
—Mrs. Sandra Green, Monte Vista, Colorado

APPLE SCOTCH PIE

9 or 10-inch unbaked pie shell	4 tablespoons flour
6 to 8 tart apples	1/8 teaspoon salt
1-1/2 cup brown sugar	1 teaspoon butter
1 cup water	1 teaspoon vanilla
2 teaspoons vinegar	

Peel, core and slice apples. Heat half of sugar with water and vinegar. Add apples and simmer until tender. Remove apples from syrup with a slotted spoon. Mix remaining sugar with flour and salt. Add slowly to syrup and cook until thickened. Remove from stove, add butter and vanilla. Fill pie shell with the apples and pour the hot syrup mixture over. Cover pie with strips of pastry arranged in lattice fashion. Bake at 425⁰ for 10 minutes, then reduce heat to 375⁰ for 25 to 35 minutes. Serve warm. —Mrs. Ray Terpstra, Lynden, Washington

UPSIDE DOWN PECAN APPLE PIE

Pastry for 9- or 10-inch pie
   4 tablespoons butter, softened
2/3 cup pecan halves
2/3 cup brown sugar, firmly
   packed
  6 cups apples, sliced

1/2 cup brown sugar, firmly
   packed
  1 tablespoon flour
1/2 teaspoon cinnamon
1/4 teaspoon nutmeg
1/4 teaspoon salt

Spread the butter evenly over the bottom and sides of the pie plate. Stand nuts, round side down, about 1 inch apart around edge of pie plate. With remaining nuts, make design in bottom. Press nuts into butter to hold in place. Sprinkle the 2/3 cup brown sugar over the nuts, pat gently but firmly, being careful not to disarrange nuts. Cover sugar-nut layer with plain pastry. Trim, leaving about 1/2 inch overhang around edge of pie plate. Set aside while preparing filling. Pare, core and slice enough apples to make the 6 cups. Sprinkle with lemon juice to prevent fruit from discoloring. In a bowl combine the 1/2 cup brown sugar and the remaining ingredients and mix with the apples. Place in the prepared pie shell and cover with pastry. Trim the top crust to match the bottom crust, fold edges together, and flute. Pierce the top crust with a fork in several places to allow steam to escape. Bake at 450° for 10 minutes, then reduce heat to 350° and bake for 30 to 45 minutes more until apples are tender and pastry is golden brown. Remove from oven and place on a rack to cool for 10 minutes. Place a serving plate over pie and invert. Carefully remove the pie plate and serve warm either plain or with butter pecan or vanilla ice cream.

—Mrs. Marion Staats, Sturgeon Bay, Wisconsin

SWEDISH APPLE NUT PIE

1/2 cup flour	1/4 cup brown sugar
1 teaspoon baking powder	1 tablespoon butter, melted
1/4 teaspoon salt	1 teaspoon vanilla
2 eggs	1 cup apples, sliced
1/4 cup sugar	1 cup pecans, chopped

Combine the flour, baking powder and salt. In a bowl, beat the eggs and gradually add the sugars and butter. Stir in the vanilla and the flour mixture. Fold in the apples and nuts. Turn into a buttered 9-inch pie plate and bake at 350° for 35 minutes. This pie does not have a crust!
—*Mrs. Gordon Amstutz, Apple Creek, Ohio*

FRESH BERRY PIE

1 9-inch pie shell, baked	2 tablespoons cornstarch
1 cup sugar	3 tablespoons fruit-flavored gelatin
1 cup water	1 quart fresh berries or fruit

In a saucepan, boil together the sugar, water and cornstarch until thick and transparent, about 10 minutes. Add the flavor of gelatin to correspond with the flavor of the berries or fruit that you are using. Fold in the fruit and pour into the baked pie shell. Refrigerate. Serve with whipped cream.   —*Harriet Johnson, Cambridge, Minnesota*

FLAVOR TWISTS: *Sprinkle 1 tablespoon lemon flavored gelatin over your next apple pie before putting on the top crust. The flavor is delicious and the gelatin helps prevent the juice from running over as the pie bakes. Adding cherry flavored gelatin to cherry pie is also tasty, but raspberry with cherry pie is unusually great.* Mrs. Charles Landphair, Humeston, Iowa

PICHERPLE PIE

1 9-inch pie shell, unbaked
1 can cherry pie filling
2 cups apples, sliced
2 tablespoons pineapple, crushed
2 tablespoons tapioca

1 tablespoon cornstarch
3/4 cup sugar
1/4 teaspoon cinnamon
Dash of nutmeg
1 teaspoon butter

Mix the ingredients all together and pour into the pie shell. A couple drops of red food coloring may be added. Bake at 400° for 10 minutes. Reduce heat to 375° for 20 minutes.

—*Kae Dailie, Milbank, South Dakota*

CHERRY PIE

2 cups graham crackers, crushed
1/4 cup butter, melted
1/4 teaspoon cinnamon
1/4 cup sugar
11 ounces cream cheese

1/2 cup sugar
2 egg yolks
1-1/2 teaspoon vanilla
1 can cherry pie filling

Combine the graham cracker crumbs, butter, cinnamon and sugar and press into a 9-inch pie pan. Cream together the cream cheese, sugar, egg yolks and vanilla. Spread over the crust. Pour the cherry filling over the cheese layer and refrigerate.

—*Mrs. Gary Vande Voort, Leighton, Iowa*

PERFECT MERINGUE: *Use a teaspoon of corn starch for each egg white. Mix with the sugar and add to the egg whites, beating until all the sugar is dissolved. Bake at 325° for 20 minutes or until browned. The slower temperature allows the meringue to dry out and stay fluffy.*   *Mrs. Loren W. Hurst, Milo, Iowa*

CHERRY PIE SUPREME

1 9-inch pie shell, baked
1 #2 can sour cherries (2 cups)
3 tablespoons cornstarch
3/4 cup sugar
1/8 teaspoon salt
1/4 teaspoon cinnamon

1 cup evaporated milk
2 tablespoons butter, melted
1 tablespoon lemon juice
Dash of salt
1 cup powdered sugar

Chill the evaporated milk in ice tray in the freezer until ice crystals form. Drain the cherries and add enough water to make 1 cup of juice. In a saucepan, combine the cornstarch, sugar, 1/8 teaspoon salt and cinnamon. Gradually add the cherry juice, stirring until smooth. Cook and stir over medium heat until thick. Set aside to cool. Mix until smooth the butter, lemon juice, dash of salt and powdered sugar. In a small, deep bowl, which has been chilled in the refrigerator, beat the chilled milk until fluffy. Add the powdered sugar mixture and beat until fluffy. Add the cherries to the cooled cornstarch mixture and pour into the baked pie shell. Cover with the whipped milk. Chill for several hours before serving.

—Mrs. Helen Bausch, Mayetta, Kansas

CONCORD GRAPE PIE

1 9-inch pie shell, unbaked
3-1/2 cups blue Concord grapes
1 cup sugar

4 tablespoons flour
1/4 teaspoon lemon juice
1 teaspoon butter

Remove grapes from stems, wash and measure. Slip skins from grapes. Place skins in a covered bowl to prevent drying out. Over medium heat, bring pulp to boil, stirring occasionally to prevent sticking. When seeds are loose, remove from heat. Press pulp through sieve to remove seeds. Combine seedless pulp with grape skins, add lemon juice and sugar mixed with flour. Fill 9-inch crust and dot with butter. Cover with lattice crust, lightly sprinkle with sugar. Bake at 375° for 50 minutes. Serve warm with ice cream.   *—Mrs. Harold Wheat, San Jose, Illinois*

CRANBERRY DATE PIE

1 8-inch pie shell, baked
1-1/2 cup cranberries
1 cup water
1/4 teaspoon soda
1 cup sugar

2 tablespoons flour
1/2 cup dates, chopped
1/2 cup nuts, chopped
1/2 teaspoon vanilla

Cook cranberries, water and soda until tender. Combine the sugar and flour, stir into the cranberries. Add the dates. Cook until clear then add the nuts and vanilla. Cool. Pour into the baked pie shell and top with whipped cream. — *Mrs. Hilda Thelen, Pewamo, Michigan*

JAPANESE FRUIT PIE

1 8-inch pie shell, unbaked
1 cup sugar
2 eggs
1/2 cup butter, melted

1/2 cup coconut
1/2 cup pecans
1/2 cup raisins
1 tablespoon vinegar

Mix together the sugar, eggs and butter. Add the rest of the ingredients and pour into the pie shell. Bake at 300° for about 40 minutes.

—*Judy Payne, Centerburg, Ohio*

PINEAPPLE-PEACH RAISIN PIE

1 9-inch pie shell, unbaked
2-1/2 cups peaches, sliced
1/2 cup peach syrup
1/2 cup white sugar
1/4 cup brown sugar, firmly
packed

3/4 cup crushed pineapple,
well drained
1/4 cup raisins
1 tablespoon lemon juice
2-1/2 tablespoons tapioca
1/2 teaspoon salt

In mixing bowl, combine sugars, peach syrup, salt, lemon juice and tapioca. Mix well. Add pineapple and raisins. Mix well. Add peaches and pour into the pie shell, arranging peaches to distribute well. Top with crust and bake at 400° for 40 to 45 minutes.

—*Mrs. Richard Feltman, Chamberlain, South Dakota*

PEAR PIE

1 9-inch pie shell, unbaked
2 cups fresh pears (about 3 large)
1/2 cup sugar
2 tablespoons flour
1/2 teaspoon salt
1 egg, beaten
1 cup sour cream
1/2 teaspoon vanilla
1/2 cup brown sugar
2/3 cup flour
1/4 teaspoon nutmeg
1/4 teaspoon cinnamon
1/3 cup butter

Peel, core and thinly slice the pears. Mix the 1/2 cup sugar, flour, salt, egg, sour cream and vanilla. Pour over the pears and put into the unbaked pie shell. Sprinkle with a little nutmeg and bake in a hot oven, 425°, for 15 minutes. Meanwhile prepare the crumb topping. In a small bowl mix the brown sugar, flour and spices. Cut in the butter and mix with your fingers until mixture holds together to form crumbs. Take pie from the oven, reduce the oven heat to 350°. Sprinkle the crumb topping over the pie, return to oven and bake for 40 to 60 minutes or until knife comes out clean when inserted in the center of the pie.

—Stella Beyer, Woodburn, Oregon

PRUNE APRICOT DELITE PIE

1 9-inch pie shell, unbaked
1-1/2 cup prunes, cooked
1-1/2 cup dried apricots, cooked
2 eggs
1/2 cup granulated sugar
1/8 teaspoon salt
1/2 cup prune juice
1/2 cup cream or condensed milk
1 tablespoon butter, melted
1 tablespoon flour

Streusel Topping
1/4 cup brown sugar
3 tablespoons butter
1/4 teaspoon cinnamon
1/2 cup flour

Chop the drained prunes into large pieces. Drain the apricot halves (may use canned apricots, but the flavor isn't as good). In a bowl combine the eggs and the next six ingredients and mix well, then add the fruit. Pour into the unbaked pie shell and top with the streusel which has been combined and rubbed together using the finger tips. Bake in a 425° oven for 35 to 40 minutes.

—Mrs. Rita M. Bianchi, Northford, Connecticut

RHUBARB CHERRY PIE

1 9-inch pie shell, unbaked
2 cups rhubarb, diced
3/4 cup sugar

1 can cherry pie filling
2-1/2 tablespoons tapioca

Mix all ingredients and let stand for 15 minutes. Put in pie shell, lattice the top crust and bake at 400° for 45 minutes.

—*Viola E. Lundeberg, River Falls, Wisconsin*

GLAZED STRAWBERRY PIE

1 9-inch pie shell, baked
2-1/2 cups fresh strawberries,
halved
1 cup strawberries, crushed
3 tablespoons cornstarch

1 cup sugar
1/2 cup water
Dash of salt
Few drops red food coloring

Combine cornstarch, sugar, water and salt in a saucepan. Add crushed berries and cook over medium heat until thickened, stirring constantly. Remove from heat and add the food coloring. Arrange strawberry halves in pie shell. Pour hot mixture over berries. Chill until firm, about 3 hours. Serve with whipped cream and garnish with a berry half.

—*Mrs. Ralph Klinder, Minnesota Lake, Minnesota*

Cream Pies

APRICOT CREME

1 cup graham cracker crumbs
1/2 cup powdered sugar
1/3 cup butter, melted
2 eggs, beaten
1 cup sugar
Dash salt
1 package (8 ounces) cream
cheese, softened

2 cups canned apricot halves,
sliced
1/2 pint whipping cream
or 1 package dessert
topping, whipped
Sliced almonds, toasted

Mix together the graham cracker crumbs, powdered sugar and butter and press into a 9-inch pie plate to form crust. Set aside. In a small bowl, combine the eggs, sugar, salt and cream cheese and beat until smooth. Pour into the pie shell and bake at 325° for 35 minutes. Cool. Arrange the slices of drained apricots in a pattern covering the pie. Top with whipped cream and garnish with the toasted almonds.

—*Mrs. Albert DeBower, Allison, Iowa*

BLISSFUL BANANA PIE

1 cup vanilla wafer crumbs
1/2 cup pecans, chopped
1/3 cup butter, melted
1 package semi-sweet chocolate
pieces (6 ounces)
1/2 cup milk

3 cups miniature marshmallows
1 package vanilla pudding
(3-1/4 ounces)
1-1/2 cup milk
1/2 cup heavy cream, whipped
2 bananas, thinly sliced

Combine crumbs, nuts and butter and press into a 9-inch pie plate. Bake at 375° for 5 minutes. Cool. Combine chocolate pieces, milk and 1 cup marshmallows and melt over low heat, stirring constantly. Cool, then pour into crumb crust and chill. Combine the pudding mix with the 1-1/2 cup milk and cook until thick. Chill. Fold in whipped cream and remaining marshmallows. Arrange bananas over chocolate layer, pour marshmallow mixture over bananas. Garnish, if you wish, with additional whipped cream, banana slices and chocolate pieces.

—Betty Compton, Shelburn, Indiana

CHOCOLATE CREAM CHEESE PIE

Crust:

1-1/2 cup graham cracker crumbs
1/4 cup brown sugar

1 square unsweetened
chocolate, melted

Filling:

1 cup semi-sweet chocolate
bits, melted
6 ounces cream cheese
1/8 teaspoon salt
1/2 cup brown sugar

2 egg yolks
1 teaspoon vanilla
2 egg whites
1/4 cup brown sugar
1 cup heavy cream, whipped

Combine the crust ingredients, mix well and pat into a 9-inch pie pan. Chill. Beat together the melted chocolate bits, cream cheese and salt until fluffy. Add the brown sugar, egg yolks and vanilla and beat again until well blended and fluffy. In another bowl, combine the egg whites, and beat until soft peaks form. Add the 1/4 cup brown sugar and beat until stiff and glossy. Fold the chocolate mixture into the egg whites, then gently fold in the whipped cream. Spoon into crust and chill.

—Mrs. Eileen Strouse, Denver, Colorado

BAVARIAN MINT PIE

1 9-inch vanilla wafer
  crumb crust
2 squares unsweetened chocolate
1 bar German sweet chocolate

1/2 cup butter
3/4 cup sugar
3 eggs
1 teaspoon mint flavoring

Melt the two chocolates in a double boiler or saucepan, stirring constantly. In a small bowl beat the butter and sugar until light and fluffy, like whipped cream. In another bowl, beat the eggs until light and lemon colored. Combine the three mixtures and pour into the pie shell. Chill until firm.

—Mrs. Johnnie Kelley, Gilmore City, Iowa

BANANA SPLIT PIE

9 or 10-inch graham
  cracker crust
30 large marshmallows
1 cup milk
1 cup heavy cream, whipped

1/2 teaspoon vanilla
1 small can crushed
  pineapple, drained
1 large banana, diced
1/3 cup nuts, chopped

Melt the marshmallows and milk in a double boiler. Cool. Combine the drained pineapple, banana and nuts and fold into the melted marshmallows. Fold the whipping cream into the fruit mixture and pour into the graham crust. Refrigerate.

—Mrs. Kenneth Clasen, St. Paul, Kansas

BLUEBERRY BANANA CREAM PIE

1 9-inch pie shell, baked
  Bananas
1 can blueberry pie filling

1/2 pint heavy cream, whipped
1/4 cup pecans, chopped

Line the pie shell with two layers of bananas. Top with the blueberry pie filling and swirl the whipped cream over all. Sprinkle with chopped nuts.

—Mrs. Theodore Gruenwald, Frohna, Missouri

RASPBERRY PARTY PIE

Crust:

3 egg whites, stiffly beaten
20 soda crackers, broken
1/2 cup nuts, chopped

1 teaspoon baking powder
1-1/2 teaspoons vanilla

Filling:

8 ounces cream cheese
1/2 cup powdered sugar
1 teaspoon vanilla
1 cup raspberries

1 envelope dessert
topping mix
1 package Junket Danish
Dessert, strawberry flavor

Into the stiffly beaten egg whites, fold in the broken crackers and remaining crust ingredients. Shape into a 9-inch pie pan and bake at 325° for 20 minutes. For the filling, mix the softened cream cheese with the powdered sugar and vanilla. Whip the dessert topping mix according to the directions on the package and fold into the cream cheese mixture. Pour over the cooled meringue. Thicken the raspberries with the Junket dessert, which has also been prepared according to the directions on the package. Cool, then pour over top of pie. Chill until firm.

—*Mrs. Barbara Caywood, Arock, Oregon*

BLUEBERRY WHIP PIE

1 9-inch graham cracker crust
1 package dessert topping
1/2 cup cold milk
4 ounces cream cheese

1 cup powdered sugar
1 teaspoon vanilla
1 can blueberry pie filling

Beat the dessert topping with milk. Cream the softened cheese. Add sifted powdered sugar and vanilla. Beat well. Add to the whipped dessert topping. Pour into pie crust and refrigerate for several hours. Top with the blueberry pie filling.

—*Mrs. Aney Chatterton, Soda Springs, Idaho*

FRENCH CREAM PIE

1 package vanilla tapioca
  pudding (3-1/4 ounces)
1-1/2 cup milk
  1 tablespoon butter
  1 teaspoon almond extract

1/2 cup almonds, finely chopped
1 package frozen patty shells,
  thawed (10 ounces)
2 tablespoons confectioners'
  sugar

Combine tapioca pudding and milk in saucepan. Cook and stir over medium heat until mixture comes to a boil. Remove from heat. Stir in butter and almond extract. Cool 10 to 15 minutes, stirring twice. Cover surface with waxed paper. Chill thoroughly. Stir well, then fold in almonds. Press three thawed patty shells together. Roll out on lightly floured board into a 10-1/2-inch circle. Repeat process with remaining three shells. Place bottom of a 9-inch pie pan in center of one of the pastry circles. Lightly mark a circle, using pan bottom as a guide. Lift off pan and fill marked circle with almond-tapioca mixture. Using a pastry brush and cold water, moisten a band of pastry about 1-1/2 inches wide around filling. Place second pastry circle over top and press down around filling. Invert 9-inch pie pan over top of pastry. Cut around rim of pan with a sharp knife. Remove pan and press pastry edges together tightly to seal. Place on a chilled baking sheet. Chill ten minutes. Bake at 400° about 25 minutes or until puffed and golden. Sift confectioners' sugar over top. Increase oven temperature to highest setting. Continue baking until sugar carmelizes and top is glossy. Watch closely to prevent burning. Cool at least two hours before serving.

—Ann Hornstra, Cathlamet, Washington

HERSHEY BAR CHOCOLATE PIE

20 large marshmallows
 4 (15 cent size) Hershey bars,
   plain or with almonds
2/3 cup milk

1 cup whipping cream, whipped
8-inch pie shell, plain crust
  or graham cracker

Combine marshmallows, chocolate bars and milk in a double boiler. Melt thoroughly, stirring often. Cool. Fold in the whipped cream and pour into the pie shell. Chill several hours.

—Mrs. Denny Rowell, Berne, Indiana

HEAVENLY CHOCOLATE PIE

1 9-inch pie shell, baked
2 egg whites
1/2 teaspoon vinegar
1/4 teaspoon cinnamon
1/4 teaspoon salt
1/2 cup sugar

1 6-ounce package semi-sweet
  chocolate bits
2 egg yolks
1/4 cup water
1 cup heavy cream, whipped
1/4 cup sugar
1/4 teaspoon cinnamon

Beat together the egg whites, vinegar, cinnamon and salt until stiff, but not dry. Gradually add the 1/2 cup sugar and beat until very stiff. Spread meringue over bottom and sides of the baked pie shell. Bake at 325° for 15-18 minutes, or until lightly browned. Cool. For the filling, in a saucepan melt the chocolate chips. Blend in the egg yolks and water and stir until smooth. Spread 3 tablespoons of this mixture over the meringue. Chill the remainder until it begins to thicken. Beat the heavy cream, sugar and cinnamon until thick, spread half of it over the chocolate layer in the pie shell. Fold the chilled chocolate mixture into remaining whipped cream and spread over the pie. Chill at least 4 hours before serving.

—Mrs. Lloyd W. Law, Jr., Savanna, Illinois

FROZEN CRANBERRY VELVET PIE

1-1/4 cup graham cracker crumbs
6 tablespoons butter, melted
8 ounces cream cheese, softened
1 cup heavy cream, whipped

1/4 cup sugar
1/2 teaspoon vanilla
1 16-ounce can cranberry
  sauce

Combine crumbs and melted butter and press into a 9-inch pie pan. Fold the powdered sugar into the whipped cream. Beat the softened cream cheese until fluffy and gradually add the whipped cream, beating until smooth and creamy. Fold the cranberry sauce into the creamed mixture and spoon into the crust. Freeze. Remove from the freezer about 10 minutes before serving.

—Mrs. David E. Grube, Croton, Ohio

COCONUT CREAM PIE 3-87 good

1 9-inch pie shell, baked
1-1/4 cup milk
1/2 cup sugar
1/2 teaspoon salt
1/4 cup flour
2 tablespoons cornstarch
1/2 cup milk
2 egg yolks

1 egg
2 egg whites
1/4 cup sugar
1 tablespoon butter
1 teaspoon vanilla
1/2 cup heavy cream
2 tablespoons confectioners'
   sugar
1/2 cup toasted coconut

In a saucepan combine the first three ingredients and heat to a boil. In a bowl combine the flour and cornstarch, blend in the 1/2 cup milk and stir until smooth. Add the egg yolks and 1 egg to the flour mixture and beat until smooth. In a small bowl beat the egg whites until stiff, gradually adding the sugar while continuing to beat until egg whites are stiff and glossy. Into the saucepan with the hot milk mixture, slowly add the flour egg batter. Return to heat, stirring constantly. Cook until thick, about 5 minutes. Add the butter and vanilla. Cool slightly then slowly fold into the egg white meringue. Pour into the pie shell and refrigerate until cool. Whip the heavy cream which has been sweetened with the confectioners' sugar until stiff. Top the cooled pie with the whipped cream and sprinkle with the toasted coconut.

—Mrs. Francis V. Jacobs, Regina, Montana

GRASSHOPPER PIE

1-1/2 cup chocolate wafer crumbs
2 tablespoons butter
2/3 cup half and half cream
24 marshmallows

2 tablespoons green creme de
   menthe
2 tablespoons white creme de
   cocoa
1/2 pint heavy cream, whipped

Combine crumbs and butter and press into an 8-inch pie pan. Bake at 350° for 10 minutes. In a saucepan, combine the marshmallows and half and half cream and heat until melted. Cool. Into the marshmallow mixture, fold in the liquers and whipped cream, pour into the pie crust and freeze. Remove pie from freezer 15 to 20 minutes before serving.

—Mrs. David Mell, Waunakee, Wisconsin

HEATH BAR PIE

1 9-inch pie shell, baked
1 3-ounce box instant vanilla
  pudding
1 package dessert topping mix

2 cups cold milk
2 Heath bars, about 1/2 cup,
  crushed

Whip until stiff the pudding, Dream Whip and milk. Fold in the crushed bars and pour into the pie shell. Chill.

—Mrs. Kenneth Riskedal, Leland, Illinois

LUSCIOUS STRAWBERRY PIE

2-1/2 quarts strawberries
1-1/3 cup powdered sugar

1-1/2 pint whipping cream, whipped
9-inch pie shell, baked

Sprinkle enough powdered sugar in bottom of crust to cover generously. The berries should be fresh, whole and cleaned. Using 1 cup of berries at a time, layer on the bottom close together, but not too tightly so that juice does not seep from berries. Sprinkle the layer of strawberries generously with powdered sugar to cover well. Do this alternately, berries then powdered sugar until both are used up, piling up to resemble a cake, or if desired, a tree shape. Dessert should be about 15 inches high. Whip the cream stiff (do not use a substitute) and frost the entire dessert. Refrigerate. The secret of this dessert is that it takes about 40 minutes for the powdered sugar to "cement" the berries together. If you have a pedestal cake plate, place the strawberry dessert on it and use as a centerpiece through the meal. At serving time, slice with a sharp, wet knife.

—Marilyn Iott, Petersburg, Michigan

MINIATURE PIES: *Save the round metal margarine tubs for use as individual pie pans. On pie baking day, bake one or two tiny pies for the lunch pails, or your husband's field lunch. Snap on the plastic lids and freeze. The pies thaw out in the dinner pail in time for lunch.* Mrs. Darryl Hofer, Onida, South Dakota

PINEAPPLE SOUR CREAM PIE

9-inch pie shell, baked
1 20-ounce can pineapple,
  crushed
1/2 cup sugar
1-1/2 tablespoon cornstarch

Dash of salt
1 cup sour cream
3 egg yolks, slightly beaten
1 tablespoon lemon juice

Drain pineapple, reserving 1/2 cup juice. Combine sugar, cornstarch and salt in saucepan. Stir in crushed pineapple, reserved juice, sour cream, egg yolks and lemon juice. Cook over medium heat, stirring constantly until mixture boils and is thick. Cover pan and cool to lukewarm. Pour into the baked pie shell. Top with meringue *or* whipped cream. Meringue: Beat the 3 egg whites, 1/4 teaspoon cream of tartar and 1/8 teaspoon salt until soft peaks form. Add 6 tablespoons sugar gradually, beating well after each addition. Continue beating until meringue stands in stiff peaks. Bake the meringue topped pie at 350° for 12-15 minutes or until the meringue is lightly browned.

—Mrs. F. J. Folta, Hawk Point, Missouri

OLD-FASHIONED CREAM PIE

1 9-inch pie shell, unbaked
1 pint cream
1 cup sugar

1 teaspoon vanilla
4 egg whites

Beat egg whites stiff then fold into the combined cream, sugar and vanilla mixture. Pour into the unbaked pie shell and bake at 425° for 10 minutes. Reduce heat to 325° and continue to bake for 30-35 minutes. Serve cold. Sprinkle top with nutmeg or sprinkle top with coconut and slip under the broiler for a few seconds to just brown. Watch it carefully.

—Mrs. Sharon Fimian, Alma, Wisconsin

SOUR CREAM APPLE PIE

1 9-inch pie shell, unbaked
2 cups apples, unpeeled, cut fine
2 tablespoons flour
1/2 teaspoon salt

3/4 cup sugar
1 egg
1 cup sour cream
1/2 teaspoon vanilla

Sift dry ingredients together. Add egg, cream and vanilla. Beat until smooth. Add apples and mix well. Pour into crust and bake at 400° for 15 minutes. Reduce heat to 350° and continue to bake for 30 to 40 minutes. **Topping:** Combine 1/3 cup sugar, 1/3 cup flour, 1 teaspoon cinnamon and 1/4 cup butter. Mix into crumbs and sprinkle over hot pie. Return pie to oven and bake at 400° for 10 minutes.

—*Mrs. Herb Harrison, Menomonie, Wisconsin*

STRAWBERRY ANGEL PIE

3 egg whites
1/4 teaspoon cream of tartar
    Dash of salt
3/4 cup sugar
2 packages (10-ounce)
    frozen strawberries

1 box (3-ounce) strawberry
    flavored gelatin
3 ounces cream cheese
1 tablespoon lemon juice
1 cup heavy cream, whipped

Butter bottom and sides of 9-inch pie pan. Beat egg whites, salt and cream of tartar until stiff but not dry. Add sugar, 1 tablespoon at a time and beat until stiff. Spread and shape into the pie pan to form crust. Bake in a 275° oven for 1-1/2 hours. Turn off oven and cool with door closed for several hours. Drain berries, reserve syrup. Add water to syrup to make 1 cup. Heat to boiling and pour over gelatin, stirring until dissolved. Soften the cream cheese. Add the lemon juice then gradually beat in the gelatin, mixing well until cheese in dissolved into the gelatin. Chill until partially set; add the berries. Fold in the whipped cream, chill again until partially set and pour into the meringue shell. Chill well.

—*Mrs. John P. Gallahue, Piper City, Illinois*

STRAWBERRY QUEEN'S PIE

Crust:
 1/2 cup butter   1 cup flour
 2 tablespoons powdered sugar

Filling:
 1 5-ounce box vanilla pudding   1 cup sugar
2-3/4 cups milk   3 tablespoons cornstarch
 4 cups fresh strawberries   1/4 cup water
 1 tablespoon lemon juice   1 cup heavy cream, whipped

Mix as for pie crust the butter, powdered sugar and flour. Pat into the bottom of a 9-inch pie pan. Bake at 350° for about 15 minutes, or until crust is golden brown. Cool. Prepare the pudding using the 2-3/4 cups milk. Cool. Cut 2 cups of berries into halves. Crush the remaining 2 cups, add the lemon juice, sugar mixed with the cornstarch and water. Bring this mixture to a boil and cook until thickened. Cool slightly. Reserve about 1/4 cup of the halved berries for garnish and add remainder to the cooked berries. Pour into the pie shell and refrigerate. At serving time, cover with the whipped cream and garnish with chopped nuts and strawberries.

—Mrs. Mary Van Wyk, Sully, Iowa

SIMPLE SUMMER PIE

 3 cups sugar coated cornflakes   1/2 pint heavy cream, whipped
 3 ounces nuts, chopped   3-1/2 ounces instant pudding,
1/3 cup butter   any flavor
 2 tablespoons sugar   1 cup cold milk

Crush corn flakes to measure 1 cup crumbs. Combine crumbs and nuts and add the butter, which has been melted with the sugar. Reserve 2 tablespoons of the crumb mixture for topping. Press into a 9-inch pie pan. Chill. Beat the pudding mix and milk for 1 minute. Gently fold in the whipped cream and spread evenly into the chilled crust. Garnish with the 2 tablespoons crumbs and refrigerate about 2 hours.

—Mrs. Kenneth D. Schoen, Pittsford, New York

STRAWBERRY BANANA PIE

1 8-inch pie shell, baked
1 banana
1 package frozen strawberries,
  whole

1 cup sugar
1 cup water
2 tablespoons cornstarch
2 tablespoons lemon juice

Mix sugar, water, cornstarch and lemon juice. Cook until thick. Cool. Slice banana into the pie shell. Cover with the strawberries. Pour cooled, cooked mixture over fruit. Cool until set. Top with sweetened whipped cream.   —*Mrs. Lois Beavers, Big Cabin, Oklahoma*

> **RED HOTS**: *A few red cinnamon candies added to rhubarb pie or sauce give it a nice pink color and added flavor.*
>   Mrs. John Hein, Columbus, Wisconsin

STRAWBERRY CHANTILLY

1 9-inch pie shell, unbaked
1/4 cup butter
1 cup sugar
3 tablespoons flour
3 eggs, separated
1/2 cup lemon juice

1-1/2 cup milk
1/2 cup sour cream
1/2 cup heavy cream, whipped
1 pint fresh strawberries <u>or</u>
  1 16-ounce package frozen
  berries, sliced

Cream butter, add sugar and flour, mixing well. Add egg yolks and beat until light. Add lemon juice and slowly blend in the milk. Fold in the stiffly beaten egg whites. Turn into the pie shell and bake at 450° for 15 minutes. Reduce heat to 325° for 20 to 25 minutes. Cool completely. If using fresh strawberries, slice the clean berries, sprinkle with a small amount of sugar and cover top of pie. If using the frozen berries, drain the juice and add 2 tablespoons cornstarch. Cook until thickened, then add the berries. Cool and cover pie with berry mixture. Top with the whipped cream into which you have gently folded the sour cream.   —*Mrs. Florann Young, Meridian, Idaho*

RHUBARB CREAM PIE

1 9-inch pie shell, unbaked
3 cups rhubarb, diced
1-1/2 cup sugar
3 tablespoons flour
1/2 teaspoon nutmeg
1 tablespoon butter
2 eggs, well beaten

In a bowl combine the eggs, sugar, flour, nutmeg and butter. Put the rhubarb into the pie shell and pour the egg mixture over the fruit. Cover with crust, or cut fancy shapes to put on top of the fruit. Bake at 450° for 10 minutes, then reduce heat to 350° for 30 minutes.

—*Mrs. Elden K. Ewalt, Knox City, Missouri*

SPECIAL ORANGE PIE

Crust:

3 egg whites, beaten
1 cup sugar
1/4 teaspoon baking powder
1 teaspoon vanilla
14 soda crackers, rolled fine
1/2 cup nuts, chopped

Filling:

1 can (6 ounces) frozen orange
juice (thawed)
1 can sweetened condensed
milk (13-1/2 ounces)
1 small carton Cool-whip

For the crust, gradually add the sugar to the beaten egg whites, beating until stiff and glossy. Add the baking powder and vanilla. Fold in the soda crackers and nuts. Butter rim and bottom of a 9-inch pie plate, press crust into pan and bake at 325° for 30 minutes. Cool. For the filling, combine the orange juice, condensed milk and Cool-whip. Pour into the baked shell and chill. Serve with a garnish of whipped cream and mandarin oranges.

—*Mrs. Martha Meisinger, Plattsmouth, Nebraska*

FLAKY CRUST: *To prevent the bottom crust of your fruit pies from becoming soggy, brush it with egg white before filling.*
Mrs. Joe Hotterman, Loose Creek, Missouri

Chiffon Pies

PINK BIRTHDAY PIE

1 9-inch pie crust, baked
1 10-ounce package frozen
  strawberries, thawed
1 cup sugar

1 teaspoon lemon juice
1/2 teaspoon salt
2 egg whites
1 cup whipping cream, whipped

In a large bowl place the strawberries, juice included, sugar, lemon juice, salt and egg whites. Beat with an electric mixer using the medium speed to combine all the ingredients, then turn to high speed and beat for 15 or more minutes until mixture is stiff and frothy. Fold in the whipping cream and pile high into the baked pie shell. Freeze until serving time. Remove from freezer and allow to soften slightly at room temperature at least 15 minutes before serving.

—Mrs. John L. Kost, Moorhead, Minnesota

36

CHOCOLATE CRUSTED CHIFFON PIE

Crust

1-1/4 cup flour
1/3 cup sugar
1/4 cup cocoa
1/2 teaspoon salt

1/2 cup shortening
1/2 teaspoon vanilla
2 to 3 tablespoons cold water

Filling

1 envelope unflavored gelatin
1/4 cup milk
4 eggs, separated
1-1/4 cup milk
1/3 cup sugar

1/2 teaspoon salt
1 teaspoon vanilla
1/4 cup sugar
1 cup whipping cream

In a bowl combine the flour, sugar, cocoa and salt. Cut in the shortening until particles are the size of small peas. Sprinkle with 2 or 3 tablespoons water, add the vanilla and toss until dough forms. Roll the dough between two pieces of waxed paper to make an 11 or 12-inch circle. Fit pastry into a 9-inch pie plate, trim off excess dough and flute the edge of the pie crust. Prick crust with fork. Place the dough trimming in a second pan and bake the crust and trimmings in a 400° oven for 8 to 10 minutes. *Do Not Overbake.* Cool. Crumble the cooled trimmings and save for crumb topping. For the pie filling, soften the gelatin in the cold milk. In a saucepan combine the egg yolks, slightly beaten, the milk, sugar and salt. Cook over medium heat, stirring constantly, until mixture thickens and coats a spoon. Remove from heat, add vanilla and the softened gelatin and stir until well dissolved. Chill until mixture begins to thicken. Beat the egg whites until stiff and gradually beat in the 1/4 cup sugar and continue beating until stiff peaks form. Fold the egg white meringue into the gelatin mixture and pour into the chocolate crust. Chill for several hours. At serving time, top with the whipped cream and sprinkle with the chocolate crumbs.

—*Mrs. Tom Blum, Morrill, Nebraska*

"MELTS ON THE FOIL": *When melting chocolate chips I fix some aluminum foil over the edges of a pan of water for a disposable double boiler. Saves a sticky pan and it's easy to just scrape off the melted chocolate with a rubber spatula.*

Sally Stauber, Milwaukee, Wisconsin

LEMONADE PIE

1 9-inch pie shell, baked
1 cup frozen lemonade, thawed
3 egg yolks
2 teaspoons unflavored gelatin

3 egg whites
1/4 teaspoon cream of tartar
1/2 cup sugar
1 cup heavy cream, whipped

In a saucepan, combine the lemonade, egg yolks and gelatin. Cook, stirring constantly until mixture boils and coats a metal spoon. Place pan in refrigerator and allow mixture to mound softly. (Do not allow it to get too stiff.) Beat egg whites and cream of tartar until frothy and soft peaks form. Add the sugar gradually, beating until stiff. Fold the egg whites and whipped cream into the lemonade mixture and mound into the pie shell. Note: a graham cracker pie shell may be used.

—Mrs. Ralph Stauffacher, Sun Prairie, Wisconsin

SESAME SEED PIE

Crust

1/4 cup sesame seeds, toasted
1 cup flour
1/2 teaspoon salt

1/3 cup oil
2 to 3 tablespoons milk

Filling

1 package unflavored gelatin
1/4 cup cold water
1 cup milk
1/4 cup sugar
2 egg yolks

1/4 teaspoon salt
2 egg whites
2 tablespoons sugar
1 cup heavy cream, whipped
1/2 cup dates, diced

In a 325° oven toast the sesame seeds for 8 minutes. Add the seeds to the flour, salt, oil and milk. Form dough into ball and roll between waxed paper to fit an 8-inch pie pan. Prick and bake at 425° for 10 minutes or until golden. Dissolve gelatin in the cold water. Set aside. In a saucepan combine the milk, sugar, egg yolks and salt and cook slowly until mixture boils and coats a metal spoon, stirring constantly. Add gelatin and stir until dissolved. Chill in refrigerator until almost set. Meanwhile beat the egg whites and 2 tablespoons sugar until a meringue. Into the gelatin mixture gently fold in the meringue, whipped cream and dates. Mound into the pie shell, sprinkle with nutmeg and chill until serving time.

—Mrs. Marlene Reed, Hales Corners, Wisconsin

FRESH COCONUT CHIFFON PIE

Coconut Pie Shell

*1/3 cup fresh coconut,
    1/2 inch cubes
1-1/2 cup flour

1/2 cup shortening
3 tablespoons cold water

Filling

1/4 cup cold water
1-1/2 envelopes unflavored
    gelatin
3 tablespoons boiling water
4 eggs, separated

1 teaspoon vanilla
1/4 teaspoon salt
3/4 cup sugar
**1 cup coconut, cubed

Put coconut in blender container, cover and run on low until coconut is finely grated. Set aside. Mix the flour and salt in a medium bowl, cut in shortening until the size of peas. Mix coconut with flour. Sprinkle water over all. Mix with a fork until dough holds together. Roll out and fit into a 10-inch pie pan. Prick bottom of shell with fork. Bake at 450° for 12 to 15 minutes. *Shredded coconut may be used, 1/2 cup for shell. **Filling:** Soften gelatin in cold water and let stand in blender container until gelatin is moistened. Add boiling water, cover and run on low until gelatin is dissolved. While continuing to run, add egg yolks one at a time. Stop blender, add vanilla, salt and 1/2 cup sugar. Cover and run on high until smooth. Add coconut, cover and run on low until coconut is finely grated. **Shredded coconut—1-1/3 cup. Chill in refrigerator until mixture begins to thicken. In a medium bowl, beat the egg whites until soft peaks form. Gradually add remaining 1/4 cup sugar and beat until stiff. Fold the chilled coconut mixture into beaten egg whites. Pour into pie shell. Chill until firm. Top with sweetened whipped cream and mandarin orange sections.

—Diane Woker, Okawville, Illinois

EASY FIT: *If you find it difficult to put your pie crust into your pie pan, simply roll the dough back onto your rolling pin. Then just put it over the pan, unroll it and shape into the pan.*
Mrs. Dean Jones, Reading, Kansas

COCONUT PEACH CHIFFON PIE

1 graham cracker crust
1 cup canned peaches, diced,
   drained (Reserve syrup)
1 tablespoon lemon juice

1 3-ounce package orange
   flavored gelatin
1 package whipped
   dessert topping
3/4 cup coconut

Combine the reserved peach syrup with enough water to measure 1-3/4 cup. Heat to boiling and stir into the orange gelatin. Dissolve well and refrigerate until the gelatin reaches the syrupy stage. Then whip the gelatin using the high speed on your mixer until double in volume and frothy. Whip the dessert topping according to directions on the package and fold gently into the whipped jello. Fold in the peaches, sprinkled with the lemon juice and the coconut and pile into the graham crust.

—Mrs. Glenn Rhoads, Cedar, Michigan

CHOCOLATE PEPPERMINT CANDY PIE

1 9-inch pie shell, baked
1 envelope unflavored gelatin
1/4 cup cold water
2 eggs, separated
1-1/4 cup milk

1/2 cup peppermint candy, crushed
1/2 cup heavy cream, whipped
   Few drops red food coloring
1/8 teaspoon salt
1/4 cup sugar

Chocolate Topping

2 ounces unsweetened
   chocolate, melted
6 tablespoons butter
6 tablespoons confectioners'
   sugar

1 egg yolk
1 teaspoon water
1/4 cup pecan halves

Soften gelatin in water. Combine egg yolks with milk. Cook over low heat until mixture coats a metal spoon. Add gelatin and candy and stir until both are melted. Chill until slightly thickened. Fold in the whipped cream and food coloring. In a bowl combine the egg whites and salt. Beat until soft peaks form. Add sugar gradually and beat until stiff and glossy. Fold into peppermint mixture. Pour into pie shell and chill until firm. Spread with chocolate topping. Cream butter and sugar. Add chocolate and egg yolk. Add water and mix thoroughly. Spread over top of pie. Garnish with pecan halves. Cut with a knife that is dipped in warm water.

—Mrs. Janet Hudspeth, Greenview, Illinois

MILE HIGH LEMON PIE

1 9-inch pie shell, baked
8 eggs, separated
2 cups sugar
2 lemons

1/8 teaspoon salt
2 tablespoons unflavored gelatin
1/2 cup cold water

In a double boiler, combine the egg yolks, 1 cup sugar, the grated rind of both lemons, plus the juice of the two lemons. Add the salt and cook, stirring constantly until the consistency of thick custard, or until the liquid coats the spoon. Soak the gelatin in cold water, then add the hot custard, stirring until dissolved. Set aside to cool. Beat the egg whites stiff, but not dry. Add the remaining cup of sugar gradually, beating constantly until the sugar is dissolved and whites form stiff peaks. Fold the cooled custard carefully into the egg whites, using a wire whisk. Pile into the baked pie shell and chill for several hours. Serve with whipped cream, if desired.

—Mrs. S. J. Simonson, Badger, Iowa

SUGARPLUM PIE

1 9-inch pastry shell, baked
1 envelope unflavored gelatin
1/4 cup cold water
1 cup half and half cream
1 cup sugar
1/4 teaspoon salt

3 eggs, separated
1/3 cup maraschino cherries,
   drained, cut-up
1/3 cup coconut, shredded
1/3 cup pecans, chopped
1/2 cup heavy cream, whipped

Soften gelatin in cold water. Place half and half cream, 1/2 cup of the sugar, salt, and 3 beaten egg yolks in top of double boiler. Cook over hot water, stirring constantly until mixture coats a metal spoon. Remove from heat and stir in softened gelatin. Chill until mixture begins to congeal. Beat egg whites until stiff, adding remaining 1/2 cup sugar gradually. Beat gelatin mixture until fluffy. Fold in egg white mixture, cherries, coconut, nuts and whipped cream. Put in pie crust. Garnish with cherries and pecans. Chill. Makes 6 to 8 servings.

—Mrs. John Slichenmyer, Olney, Illinois

CHOCOLATE BAVARIAN PIE ON A CLOUD

Meringue Shell

2 egg whites
Pinch of salt
1/8 teaspoon cream of tartar

1/2 teaspoon vanilla
7 tablespoons sugar

Chocolate Bavarian Filling

1 envelope unflavored gelatin
1/4 cup cold water
1 cup light cream
    or evaporated milk
1/2 cup white corn syrup
3 eggs, separated

1/4 teaspoon salt
2 ounces unsweetened
    chocolate, melted
1 teaspoon vanilla
1/3 cup sugar

Beat the egg whites until frothy then add the salt and cream of tartar. Beat until stiff but not dry. Add the vanilla and continue beating, adding 1 tablespoon of sugar at a time until dissolved and stiff peaks form. Spread on bottom and sides of a 9-inch greased pie plate. Bake in a slow oven, 275°, for 1 hour. Turn off heat and leave in oven until cool. **Filling:** Soften gelatin in cold water. Scald cream. Beat egg yolks, blend in corn syrup and salt and beat well. Add cooled, melted chocolate and pour warm cream slowly over the egg, chocolate mixture, blending thoroughly. Return mixture to top of double boiler and cook, stirring constantly until mixture is slightly thickened and will coat a spoon. Remove from heat and add the softened gelatin. Cool. Stir in vanilla. Beat egg whites until frothy, add salt and continue beating until stiff but not dry. Add the sugar gradually and beat until stiff peaks form. Fold into the cooled chocolate mixture. Refrigerate until the mixture mounds when dropped from a spoon. Turn into the meringue shell and refrigerate until firm. Serve with a garnish of whipped cream.
— *Roberta Moellenberg, Idalia, Colorado*

SHINY CRUST: *Brush top of pie crust with a mixture of 1 egg, 1 teaspoon sugar, pinch of salt and 1 teaspoon cooking oil. Bake as usual.* Mrs. Kenneth Chatterton, Soda Springs, Idaho

ANGEL LEMON PIE

4 eggs, separated	1/3 cup lemon juice
1/4 teaspoon cream of tartar	1 tablespoon lemon rind,
1 cup sugar	grated
1/2 cup sugar	1 cup heavy cream, whipped

Prepare a meringue by beating the 4 egg whites in a bowl with the cream of tartar until frothy. Gradually beat in the 1 cup of sugar until stiff peaks form. Put in a buttered 9-inch pie plate and bake 1 hour at 275°. Let cool. Meanwhile, beat the 4 egg yolks until thick and light colored. Gradually add the 1/2 cup sugar, 1/3 cup lemon juice and lemon rind. Cook in top of a double boiler, stirring constantly until thick. Cool. Spread the lemon filling over the cooled meringue crust and top with the whipped cream. Refrigerate until serving time.

—Mrs. Evelyn Huderle, East Grand Forks, Minnesota

BANANA COCONUT CHIFFON PIE

9-inch vanilla wafer pie shell	1/3 cup sugar
1 envelope unflavored gelatin	1/4 teaspoon salt
1/4 cup cold water	1/2 cup heavy cream, whipped
3 eggs, separated	1/3 cup coconut, grated
1 cup bananas, mashed	

Soften gelatin in cold water. In a double boiler, beat the egg yolks slightly and add the sugar and salt. Cook until custard thickens or until it coats a metal spoon. Add the gelatin and stir until dissolved. Cool slightly, then add the mashed bananas and chill until mixture starts to mound with a spoon. Beat the egg whites until stiff peaks form. Beat cream until stiff. Fold the egg whites, the beaten whipped cream and the coconut into the banana custard and pile into the pie shell. Refrigerate for several hours. At serving time, garnish with banana slices, maraschino cherries and additional whipped cream.

—Mrs. Ralph Klinder, Minnesota Lake, Minnesota

PINWHEEL: *Prick cutting guidelines in the top pie crust before baking. Makes for easy cutting and attractive wedges.*
Mrs. James D. Snyder, Williamstown, West Virginia

BUTTERSCOTCH WALNUT PIE

Pie shell

1/3 cup butter, softened
  3 tablespoons sugar
  1 egg yolk

1 cup flour
2 tablespoons walnuts,
  chopped fine

Butterscotch filling

  1 envelope unflavored gelatin
1/4 cup cold water
  1 6-ounce package butterscotch
    morsels
  3 ounces cream cheese,
    softened

1/2 cup milk
  3 egg yolks
  4 egg whites
1/2 cup walnuts, chopped
1/2 teaspoon rum
    flavoring, optional
1/4 cup sugar

Mix the butter and sugar until blended. Add the egg yolk and mix well. Then add the flour and nuts and work the mixture until the dough forms. Press evenly over the bottom and sides of a 9-inch pie plate. Bake at 375° for 12 to 15 minutes or until lightly browned. Cool. **Filling:** Soften gelatin in cold water. Heat the milk and egg yolks and add the gelatin, stirring until dissolved. Add the butterscotch morsels and the cheese until well blended and dissolved. Remove from heat and add the flavoring (vanilla, if you do not like the rum flavoring) and nuts. Chill until mixture begins to thicken but not set. Meanwhile, beat the egg whites until stiff but not dry. Add the sugar gradually and continue beating until stiff peaks form. Fold into the butterscotch mixture and pour into the baked pie crust. Chill. Garnish with whipped cream at serving time.

—Mrs. Emil Havrda, Howells, Nebraska

NEAT HINT: *Place a plastic lid from a used shortening can over the bottom of your flour sifter after each use. It will keep your cupboard clean.*   *Mrs. Ray Cormany, Columbia City, Indiana*

MINCEMEAT CHIFFON PIE

1 9-inch pie shell, baked
1 envelope unflavored gelatin
3/4 cup cold water
1-1/2 cup mincemeat

3 egg whites
1/3 cup sugar
1/8 teaspoon salt
1 envelope whipped topping mix

Soften the gelatin in the cold water then over medium heat, stir until dissolved. Heat the mincemeat and add the hot gelatin and stir well. Chill in the refrigerator until slightly thickened. Beat the egg whites stiff and gradually add the sugar and salt, beating until stiff and glossy. Prepare the whipped topping according to directions on the package. Fold the egg white meringue and the whipped topping into the mincemeat. Pile into the baked pie shell. Chill.

—Mrs. Johnnie Kelley, Gilmore City, Iowa

"WEEPLESS" MERINGUE: *Moisten 1 tablespoon cornstarch with about 2 teaspoons water. Stir in 1/2 cup boiling water and cook over low heat until thickened, stirring constantly. Cool. Make regular meringue then gradually beat in the cooled cornstarch until it forms peaks.*

Mrs. Robert Roach, Dearborn, Missouri

SEAL CRACKS: *If a crack appears in your pie crust while baking, seal it with a little of the meringue you are planning to top the pie with before filling.*

Mrs. Elmer Stowell, Reedsburg, Wisconsin

PUMPKIN PIE SPICE: *Instead of measuring the cinnamon, ginger and cloves for a pumpkin pie, buy a can of prepared pumpkin pie spice from your grocer's shelf.*

Mrs. Orlin Petersen, Utica, South Dakota

Custard Pies

PARADISE PUMPKIN PIE

1 9-inch pie shell, unbaked
1 8-ounce package cream cheese
1/4 cup sugar
1/2 teaspoon vanilla
1 egg
1-1/4 cup pumpkin, canned
   or cooked

1/2 cup sugar
1 teaspoon cinnamon
1/4 teaspoon ginger
1/4 teaspoon nutmeg
  Dash of salt
1 cup evaporated milk
2 eggs, slightly beaten

Combine the softened cream cheese, sugar and vanilla. Beat until fluffy then add the egg and beat again. Pour into the pastry shell. Combine the remaining pumpkin custard ingredients and mix well. Carefully pour over the cream cheese mixture in the pie shell. Bake at 350° for 65 to 70 minutes or until knife inserted in the center of the pie comes out clean. Cool. Brush with maple syrup and decorate with pecan halves.

—Mrs. Carol Abt, Blanchester, Ohio

RAISIN MERINGUE BUTTERSCOTCH PIE

Raisin Crunch Crust

3/4 cup raisins, finely chopped
1/3 cup pecans, finely chopped
1/2 cup butter, softened

1/4 cup light brown sugar,
firmly packed
1 cup flour

Blend all ingredients together. Press into greased 9-inch pie pan, prick with fork and bake at 375° for 8-10 minutes until lightly browned. Do not overbake!

Butterscotch Filling

1 cup light brown sugar
6 tablespoons cornstarch
1/2 teaspoon salt
1-1/2 cup milk
3 egg yolks, beaten

2 tablespoons butter
2 teaspoons vanilla
1 cup raisins, chopped
1 cup dairy sour cream

In saucepan, blend brown sugar with cornstarch and salt; stir in milk. Cook, stirring constantly, over moderate heat until mixture begins to thicken. Lower heat and cook until very thick, about 15 minutes, stirring constantly. Remove from heat; stir in beaten egg yolks, then cook 5 minutes longer. Remove from heat. Beat in butter and vanilla. Stir in raisins. Cover and cool until lukewarm. Stir in sour cream and turn into baked Raisin Crunch Crust. Top with meringue. **Meringue:** Beat 3 egg whites until foamy. Add 1/4 teaspoon cream of tartar and 1/8 teaspoon salt, beating to form soft peaks. Gradually beat in 6 tablespoons sugar, 2 tablespoons at a time, until sugar is completely dissolved and stiff peaks form. Bake meringue-topped pie at 400° for 8 to 10 minutes, or until meringue is set and peaked with brown. Cool pie away from drafts. Let stand until completely cold before cutting.

—Lorraine Binfet, Loyalton, South Dakota

APPLE DUMPLINGS: *Use those little pieces of left-over pie crust for an apple dumpling. Roll the dough, place sliced apples in center, add a small amount of sugar, cinnamon and a dab of butter. Seal the dough into a dumpling and place in a plastic bag and freeze. When you get enough dumplings to serve your family, pop them in the oven and you have a quick dessert!*

Mrs. Roy Maibach, Sterling, Ohio

PERFECT LEMON PIE

1 9-inch pie shell, baked
1-1/2 cup sugar
1/4 cup cornstarch
    plus 2 tablespoons
1/4 teaspoon salt
1/2 cup lemon juice

1/2 cup cold water
3 egg yolks
2 tablespoons butter
1-1/2 cup boiling water
    Grated rind of 1 lemon

Meringue

1 tablespoon cornstarch
2 tablespoons cold water
1/2 cup boiling water
3 egg whites

6 tablespoons sugar
Dash of salt
1 teaspoon vanilla

In a saucepan mix the sugar, cornstarch and salt. Stir in the lemon juice and cold water, then the beaten egg yolks, butter, rind and boiling water. Cook over medium heat until mixture boils, stirring constantly. Boil 1 minute. Pour while hot into pie shell. For the meringue, dissolve cornstarch in cold water then add boiling water. Cook until clear, stirring constantly. Set aside. Beat egg whites stiff, gradually adding sugar a tablespoon at a time. Add salt and flavoring and beat until stiff and glossy. Gradually beat in the cooled cornstarch mixture continuing to beat holding meringue to stiff peaks. Pile the meringue on to the lemon filling and bake at 375° about 8 minutes, or until lightly browned.

—Mrs. Helen R. Long, Afton, Iowa

FRENCH SILK CHOCOLATE PIE

1 8-inch pastry shell, baked
1/2 cup butter
3/4 cup sugar

2 squares baking chocolate, melted
1 teaspoon vanilla
2 eggs

Cream butter and sugar. Beat continually while adding the melted, cooled chocolate and the vanilla. Add the eggs, one at a time, beating at least five minutes after each egg. Pour into the baked shell and chill for at least 2 hours before serving. Top with whipped cream and nuts.

—Mrs. Hilbert Gerdes, Goodhue, Minnesota

BLUM'S COFFEE-TOFFEE PIE

Pastry

1 cup flour
1/2 teaspoon salt
1/3 cup shortening
1/4 cup brown sugar

3/4 cup walnuts, finely chopped
1 square unsweetened chocolate, grated
1 teaspoon vanilla

Filling

1/2 cup butter or margarine
3/4 cup sugar
1 square unsweetened chocolate, melted

2 teaspoons instant coffee
2 eggs

Topping

2 cups heavy cream
2 tablespoons instant coffee

1/2 cup confectioners' sugar

In a medium bowl combine the flour, salt, sugar, walnuts and grated chocolate. Add 1 tablespoon water (adding a bit more if needed) and vanilla. Using a fork, mix the ingredients until the dough is crumbly. Press into a well greased 9-inch pie plate and bake at 375° for 15 minutes. Cool. In a small bowl with the electric mixer at medium speed, beat the butter until creamy. Gradually add the sugar, beating until light. Blend in the chocolate and 2 teaspoons instant coffee. Add 1 egg, beat 5 minutes; add second egg, beat another 5 minutes. Pour into the pie shell. Refrigerate, covered, overnight. Next day prepare the coffee topping. In a large bowl, combine the cream with the 2 tablespoons instant coffee and the confectioners' sugar. Refrigerate for 1 hour. With the electric mixer, beat the cream mixture until stiff. Swirl over top of pie, garnish with chocolate curls and refrigerate at least 2 hours.

—Mrs. Paul Sauder, Manheim, Pennsylvania

SPLATTER-PROOF BEATING: *To prevent cream from splattering when beating, cut a circle of waxed paper larger than the bowl you are using. Punch a hole in the center and slip the stems of the beaters through, presto, you have a splatter-proof shield!*

Mrs. Russell Schroeder, Alma Center, Wisconsin

BUTTERMILK PIE

Cornmeal shell

1 cup flour

1/2 teaspoon salt

1/2 cup cornmeal

1/2 cup shortening

1/3 cup cheddar cheese, grated

1/4 cup water

Filling

3 eggs

2 cups sugar

1/4 cup butter, melted

3 tablespoons flour

1 cup buttermilk

3 tablespoons lemon juice

Combine the flour, salt and cornmeal. Cut in the shortening until mixture resembles fine crumbs. Stir in the cheese and sprinkle the water over the mixture, mixing lightly with fork. Roll to 1/8-inch thickness and line a 9-inch pie pan. Trim and flute edges. Beat eggs, add sugar and beat well. Add remaining ingredients and mix well. Pour into crust and bake at 350º for 1 hour.

—*Mrs. John P. Gallahue, Piper City, Illinois*

CARAMEL CREAM DOUBLE DECKER PIE

1-1/3 cup white sugar

2/3 cup flour

1/4 teaspoon salt

4 eggs

4 cups milk

2 teaspoons vanilla

Add 1/4 cup butter or margarine to regular pastry recipe for double crust pie. Divide dough in half. Roll each half in a square a bit thicker than for regular pie. Prick with fork. Bake on a cookie sheet in a 450º oven for 12 to 15 minutes, or until lightly browned. Melt the sugar in a heavy skillet until dark brown, stirring frequently. Do not burn. Add 1 cup milk and let simmer until the sugar is dissolved. Put 2 cups milk to heat in a double boiler. Blend flour and salt with 1 cup milk and add to the milk in the double boiler. Add the sugar mixture. Stir with a wire whisk until custard is well cooked, about 15 minutes. Slowly add the slightly beaten eggs. Cook for 3 minutes. Cool. Add vanilla. Place one crust on a flat dessert plate. Spread half of the filling over the crust. Top with second crust and spread with remaining filling. To serve; cut in squares, top with whipped cream and garnish with chopped nuts.

—*Margaret Walden Haun, Santa Cruz, California*

CARROT PIE

1 9-inch pie shell, unbaked

Filling

2 cups carrots, cooked and
    mashed
2 egg yolks (reserve egg whites)
1/2 cup brown sugar, firmly
    packed

1/2 teaspoon salt
1/4 teaspoon mace
1/4 teaspoon cinnamon
3/4 cup half and half cream
    or evaporated milk

Topping

1/2 cup brown sugar
  2 tablespoons butter

1 tablespoon flour
1/2 cup pecans, chopped

Combine the filling ingredients and mix thoroughly. Beat the two egg whites stiff and fold into the carrot mixture. Pour into the pie shell and bake at 350º for 1 hour. Meanwhile combine the topping ingredients and mix together until crumbly. Check pie to make sure the custard is set then remove from oven and sprinkle topping over the pie. Return to a 400º oven and bake for 10 minutes.

—Mrs. Mary Van Wyk, Sully, Iowa

BUTTERSCOTCH DE-LITE PIE

1/2 cup flour
1/4 cup butter
1/4 cup pecans, chopped fine
  4 ounces cream cheese
1/2 cup confectioners' sugar

1 envelope whipped dessert
    topping
1/2 cup milk
1 small box instant butterscotch
    pudding
1-1/2 cup milk

Combine the flour, butter and pecans and press into an 8 or 9-inch pie pan. Bake at 350º for 10 to 12 minutes. Whip the dessert topping with the 1/2 cup milk. Combine the cream cheese with the confectioners' sugar. Fold the two together and spread over the crust. Prepare the pudding using the 1-1/2 cup milk. Pour over the cheese layer and refrigerate. Serve with whipped cream or additional whipped dessert topping.

—Mrs. Virgil James, Cumberland, Iowa

CHOCOLATE COCONUT PIE

3 9-inch pie shells, unbaked
4 cups sugar
3 tablespoons flour
1/2 cup cocoa
Dash of salt
1/2 cup butter

6 eggs
1 tablespoon vanilla
1 large can evaporated milk
1 can coconut (4 ounces)
1 cup nuts, chopped

Mix sugar, flour, cocoa and salt. Add the butter, which has been melted, eggs and vanilla. Stir in milk, coconut and nuts. Pour into the pie shells and bake at 350° for 20-25 minutes.

—Mrs. Jo Bell, Dresden, Tennessee

COTTAGE CHEESE CUSTARD PIE

1 10-inch pie shell, unbaked
1 cup cottage cheese
Salt
1/2 cup sugar

2 tablespoons flour
2 eggs, separated
1 cup cream or evaporated milk

Mix together cottage cheese, salt, sugar, flour, egg yolks and cream. Fold in the stiffly beaten egg whites and pour into the pie shell. Bake at 375° for 1 hour. Delicious served warm with pure New York maple syrup.

—Mrs. Donald Moser, Croghan, New York

HARVEST FESTIVAL PIE

1 9-inch pie shell, unbaked
1 cup pinto bean pulp
2 egg yolks, beaten
1/2 teaspoon cinnamon
1/4 teaspoon salt
1/4 teaspoon nutmeg

1/4 teaspoon allspice
1/4 teaspoon ginger
1 teaspoon vanilla
1/2 cup brown sugar
2 tablespoons corn syrup
3/4 cup milk

Combine all ingredients and mix well. Pour into the unbaked pie shell and bake at 300° about 30 minutes, or until brown and until knife inserted near edge of custard comes out clean. Top with meringue or whipped cream.

—Irene Tombre, Savage, Montana

STRAWBERRY PIE

1 9-inch pie crust, baked
1 cup sugar
4 tablespoons strawberry
    flavored gelatin
8 teaspoons cornstarch

2 cups water
1 teaspoon red food coloring
1 quart fresh strawberries
1 3-ounce package cream cheese
Whipped topping

Combine sugar, gelatin and cornstarch in saucepan. Add water and food coloring. Cook until clear and thickened. Cool. Spread softened cream cheese on crust bottom and chill. Put chilled whole or halved berries in crust and spoon filling over them. Refrigerate pie. Add whipped topping to each piece when served. This recipe is delicious on cheese cake.

—Mrs. Glenda Walters, Charlotte, Michigan

EGG SEPARATOR: *Use a kitchen funnel for an egg separator. Place the funnel over a cup and break the egg into it. The white will slide into the cup and the yolk will be left in the funnel.*
Mrs. Edgar Buck, Babbitt, Minnesota

SUBSTITUTE SOUR CREAM: *Place 1/2 cup warm water in a small bowl; add 1 cup plus 2 tablespoons dry milk and mix well. Add 1 teaspoon vinegar gradually and mix smooth. Mixture will thicken if allowed to stand.*
Mrs. Henry Evers, Florence, Alabama

Ice Cream Pies

ICE CREAM FRUIT PIE

8-inch graham cracker pie shell
1 3-ounce package instant
  vanilla pudding
1 pint vanilla ice cream, softened

1 cup milk
2 cups crushed pineapple,
  drained
1 tablespoon cornstarch

Mix the cornstarch with 1/2 cup of the reserved juice. Add the fruit and cook until thick and clear, stirring constantly. Chill well. In a bowl, combine the pudding, milk and ice cream and beat well for a minute or two. Pour into the crust and refrigerate. Spread the fruit glaze over the chilled pie and return to refrigerator until serving time. NOTE: Fruit topping may be varied to your liking. Also, this pie keeps well for a day or two.

—*Mrs. Helen Bausch, Mayetta, Kansas*

MILLION DOLLAR CHOCOLATE PIE

1 8-inch graham cracker crust
1 pint vanilla ice cream

1 box instant chocolate pudding
   (3 ounces)
3/4 cup milk

Dissolve pudding in milk. Fold in softened ice cream. Pour into graham cracker crust. Chill. Top with chocolate curls cut from a chocolate bar.
—Mrs. Neil Loynachan, Knoxville, Iowa

RASPBERRY EXTRAVAGANZA PIE

1 cup graham cracker crumbs
3 tablespoons light brown sugar
3 tablespoons butter, melted
1 8-ounce package
   frozen raspberries
2 tablespoons sugar
   Rind of 1 lemon, grated
   Juice of 1 lemon, strained

1/2 cup cold water
1 tablespoon cornstarch
1-1/2 quart vanilla ice cream,
   slightly softened
3 egg whites
6 tablespoons sugar
   Coconut, flaked

Mix the first 3 ingredients for the pie crust and press into a 9-inch pie plate. Freeze. In saucepan, combine the berries, 2 tablespoons sugar, mixed with the cornstarch, rind, juice and water. Cook until clear and slightly thickened. Chill. Using about 1/2 of the sauce, alternate thin layers of ice cream and sauce in the pie shell. Freeze overnight. Beat egg whites until frothy, add the sugar gradually, beating until stiff and glossy. Spread the meringue over the ice cream sealing to the crust. Sprinkle with coconut. Place pie on wooden board and put in a preheated 500° oven. Bake for 2 minutes or until slightly browned, watching and timing carefully. To decorate, drizzle some of remaining sauce over pie. Serve immediately. Place remaining sauce in a small bowl to be spooned over individual servings.
—Mrs. John P. Gallahue, Piper City, Illinois

GRINDING RAISINS: *When grinding raisins for use in baking, rinse them first in boiling water and then in cold water. They will slip right through the grinder.*   Mrs. Lee Shenk, Laotto, Indiana

SUPER DESSERT

18 filled chocolate sandwich
   cookies
1/3 cup butter, melted
  2 squares unsweetened chocolate
1/2 cup sugar

1 tablespoon butter
1 small can evaporated milk
1 quart ice cream
1/2 cup pecans, chopped

Crush cookies. Add the 1/3 cup melted butter. Combine and press into a 9-inch pie plate. Cool. Melt chocolate. Stir in the sugar and 1 tablespoon butter. Add milk slowly and cook until creamy, stirring constantly. Fill the cooled pie shell with ice cream and spread the chocolate mixture over the ice cream. Sprinkle with nuts. Freeze until serving time.

—Mrs. Sonja Wilhau, Grundy Center, Iowa

TOFFEE ICE CREAM PIE

18 vanilla wafers
1/2 gallon vanilla ice cream,
   softened
  2 cups Heath toffee candy
   bars, chopped

1-1/2 cup sugar
1 cup evaporated milk
1/4 cup butter
1/4 cup light corn syrup
Dash of salt

Line the bottom and sides of a buttered 9-inch pie plate with the vanilla wafers. Spoon half of the softened ice cream over the wafer shell. Sprinkle 1/2 cup toffee bars over the ice cream, then cover with the remaining ice cream. Sprinkle the remaining cup of toffee bar pieces over the top of the pie. Wrap the pie in tin foil and store in the freezer until serving time. SAUCE: Before serving, prepare the following sauce to pour over the top of each piece of pie. Combine the sugar, milk, butter, syrup and salt. Bring to a boil over low heat, boil 1 minute. Remove from heat and stir in remaining toffee and cool.

—Mrs. Bob Waal, Oskaloosa, Iowa

DOUBLE DECKER PUMPKIN PIE

1 9-inch graham cracker pie
  shell, baked
1 pint vanilla ice cream
1 cup pumpkin, canned
3/4 cup sugar
1/2 teaspoon nutmeg

1/2 teaspoon ginger
1/2 teaspoon cinnamon
1/2 teaspoon salt
1 cup heavy cream, whipped
1/2 cup pecans, chopped

Spread softened ice cream in the bottom of the pie shell. Freeze. Combine the pumpkin, spices, sugar and salt. Fold in the whipped cream and spread over the ice cream. Sprinkle with nuts and return to the freezer. To serve, remove from freezer 15 to 20 minutes before serving. If preparing ahead of time, wrap carefully after pie has been frozen.

—Mrs. Amy Nieland, Arlington, Minnesota

HIDDEN TREASURE TARTS

1-1/2 cup flour
1/2 teaspoon salt
1/2 cup butter
1/3 cup confectioners' sugar
2 tablespoons water
1 teaspoon vanilla

1/3 cup pecans, finely chopped
6 to 8 ounces semi-sweet
  chocolate
2 tablespoons light cream
Ice cream

Cream together the butter and sugar. Blend in the water and vanilla then add the nuts, flour and salt. Mix as for pie dough. Press into muffin cups or 3-1/2-inch tart shells. Bake at 375° about 15 minutes. Should make 1 dozen shells. Combine the chocolate and cream and stir over medium heat until smooth. Line the cooled tarts with the warm melted chocolate mixture. At serving time, fill the tarts with a scoop of ice cream. Top with a maraschino cherry.

—Catherine Yoder, Belleville, Pennsylvania

Miscellaneous Pies

FUNNY CAKE PIE

1 9-inch pie shell, unbaked
1-1/4 cup cake flour
1 teaspoon baking powder
1/2 teaspoon salt
3/4 cup sugar
1/4 cup shortening
1/2 cup milk

1 teaspoon vanilla
1/4 cup butter
1/2 cup brown sugar
2 tablespoons light corn syrup
3 tablespoons water
1/2 teaspoon vanilla

Sift together flour, baking powder, salt and sugar. Put shortening in mixing bowl. Sift in dry ingredients. Add milk and vanilla, mix till all flour is dampened. Beat 2 minutes; add egg and beat 1 minute more. Pour batter into pie shell. Dribble lukewarm sauce over batter. Make sauce by combining butter, brown sugar, and corn syrup in saucepan. Cook and stir over low heat till mixture comes to a boil. Add water and bring to a boil again; boil 1 to 2 minutes. Remove from heat and stir in vanilla. After pouring sauce over batter, bake 50 to 55 minutes at 350°.

—*Mrs. Denny Rowell, Berne, Indiana*

IMPOSSIBLE PIE

4 eggs, beaten
1/4 cup butter, melted
1-1/2 cup sugar
1/2 cup flour
1/4 teaspoon salt

1/2 teaspoon baking powder
1 teaspoon vanilla
2 cups milk
1 cup coconut

Beat all ingredients together in bowl. Pour into a greased 9 or 10-inch pie plate and bake at 350° for 45 minutes. When baked, crust will be on the bottom, custard in the middle and coconut on the top.

—Mrs. Christine Kropf, Harrisburg, Oregon

MYSTERY PIE

3 egg whites
1 cup sugar
1 cup graham cracker crumbs

1 cup pecans
1 teaspoon vanilla

Beat the egg whites stiff. Add the sugar gradually, beating until meringue is stiff and glossy. Into the meringue, fold in the graham cracker crumbs and pecans, add the vanilla and pour into a greased 9-inch pie pan. Bake at 350° for 25 to 30 minutes. Cool. At serving time, top with whipped cream.

—Mrs. Lois Beavers, Big Cabin, Oklahoma

OATMEAL PIE

1 9-inch pie shell, unbaked
3 eggs
2/3 cup white sugar
1/2 cup brown sugar, firmly packed
2/3 cup oatmeal

1/4 cup butter, melted
1 teaspoon vanilla
1/2 cup dark syrup
2/3 cup coconut
1 tablespoon flour

Beat the eggs until light, add the white sugar and mix well. Then blend in the remaining ingredients and pour into an unbaked pie shell. Bake at 450° for 10 minutes, then reduce the oven temperature to 350° for 35 minutes.

—Violet Beard, Marshall, Illinois

OATMEAL 'N' CHOCOLATE PIE

1 9-inch pie shell, unbaked
3 eggs
3/4 cup brown sugar,
   firmly packed
1/3 cup dark corn syrup
1/3 cup maple-blended syrup

2 tablespoons flour
1/4 cup butter, melted
1 teaspoon vanilla
3/4 cup oatmeal, uncooked
   (not instant)
1/2 cup semi-sweet chocolate chips

In medium bowl, beat eggs with electric mixer until foamy. Gradually add sugar; beat until thick. Stir in remaining ingredients; blend well. Pour filling into pie shell. Bake at 350° for about 40 to 45 minutes (or until center of pie is firm). Cool completely. 8 servings.

RITZ CRACKER PIE

4 egg whites
1/2 teaspoon baking powder
1 cup sugar

1 teaspoon vanilla
21 Ritz crackers, rolled fine
2/3 cup pecans, ground

Beat the egg whites and baking powder until soft peaks form. Add the 1 cup sugar gradually continuing to beat until stiff and glossy. Add the vanilla. Fold the crackers and pecans into the egg whites and spread into a well buttered 9-inch pie plate piling it high on the sides to form a hollow in the center. Bake at 350° for 30 minutes. Turn off the oven heat and allow the pie to cool in the oven. At serving time, top with whipped cream.

—Elaine M. Cornwell, Evansville, Wisconsin

GREEN TOMATO PIE

1 9-inch pie shell
2 cups green tomatoes
1/2 cup raisins
1/2 teaspoon cloves
1/2 cup brown sugar
3/4 teaspoon salt

3/4 tablespoon cinnamon
1 tablespoon vinegar
1 tablespoon lemon rind, grated
1/8 teaspoon nutmeg, grated
2 tablespoons butter
2 tablespoons brown sugar

Skin and slice or chop tomatoes and add remaining ingredients. Pour into pie shell, sprinkle with brown sugar and dot with butter. Cover with top crust and bake at 375° for 45 to 50 minutes.

—Mary Kevorkian, Los Osos, California

Nut Pies

DATE PECAN PIE

1 9-inch pie shell, unbaked
2 tablespoons butter or
1/4 cup margarine, melted
1/4 cup light cream
2 tablespoons flour
3/4 cup sugar

1 teaspoon salt
1 cup dark corn syrup
2 eggs, beaten
1/2 cup pecan halves
1 cup dates, finely chopped
1 teaspoon vanilla

Into the cooled melted butter, stir in the cream and set aside. Mix the flour, sugar and salt together in a bowl, add the corn syrup and blend well. Add the eggs, cream mixture, nuts, dates and vanilla. Pour into the unbaked pie shell and bake at 400° for 15 minutes. Reduce heat to 350° and bake for 30 to 35 minutes or until filling is firm around the edges. Center should be slightly soft.

—*Mrs. Arnold G. Beyes, Vandalia, Illinois*

MAPLE PUDDING PECAN PIE

1 3-ounce package vanilla
   pudding mix (not instant)
1 cup maple syrup
3/4 cup evaporated milk

1 egg, slightly beaten
1 cup pecans, chopped
1 8-inch pie shell, unbaked

Blend pudding mix with maple syrup. Gradually stir in evaporated milk and egg. Add the pecans and pour into the pie shell. Bake at 375° until top is firm, about 35 to 40 minutes. Cool 4 hours or longer.

—Mrs. James Chambers, Mansfield, Ohio

PEANUT BUTTER PIE

1 9-inch pie shell, baked
1/2 cup peanut butter
2/3 cup powdered sugar
2/3 cup sugar (scant)
3 tablespoons cornstarch

1/2 teaspoon salt
3 cups milk, scalded
3 eggs, separated
1 tablespoon butter
1-1/2 teaspoon vanilla

Blend peanut butter and powdered sugar until mealy. Sprinkle 2/3 of the mixture over bottom of the baked pie shell. Combine the beaten egg yolks, salt, cornstarch and sugar and stir into the scalded milk. Cook until thick, stirring constantly. Add vanilla and butter and cool slightly. Pour into pie shell and top with meringue. Sprinkle remaining peanut butter mixture on top of meringue. Bake at 375° for 8 to 10 minutes, or until lightly browned. **Meringue:** Beat the 3 egg whites with 1/4 teaspoon cream of tartar and 6 tablespoons sugar until stiff and glossy.

—Mrs. Obil Myers, Fairview, Illinois

NUT SHELLING: *Store pecans in the freezer or refrigerator. They crack and shell so much easier.*
    Mrs. Harold Knueppel, Three Lakes, Wisconsin

Index

RHUBARB

Rhubarb Cherry—22
Rhubarb Cream—35

Ritz Cracker—60
Sesame Seed—38
Simple Summer—33

STRAWBERRY

Glazed Strawberry—22
Luscious Strawberry—30
Strawberry—53
Strawberry Angel—32
Strawberry Banana—34
Strawberry Chantilly—34
Strawberry Queen's Pie—33

Sugarplum—41
Super Dessert—57

TOFFEE

Blum's Coffee Toffee—49
Toffee Ice Cream—57

Tomato, Green Pie—60

More Mouth-Watering Treats

Here are our best bargains in books from Farm Wife News:

MICROWAVE MAGIC. With more women asking for microwave recipes, these proven time-saving ideas from farm and ranch wives can help you "zap-up" a tasty meal or put more spark in leftovers in just a matter of minutes. This book is filled with lots of hearty dishes that your whole family will really enjoy. Only $2.95.

COOKIE JAR COOKBOOK. An empty cookie jar at your house will tempt you to try some of the "familiar favorites" and "something different" recipes in this wonderful collection of recipes. Cookies are favorites with farm families as evidenced by the 2,500 recipes submitted to our cookie recipe contest by FWN readers! More than 150 of the *best* make it a great book! Only $2.95.

RECIPES FOR LEFTOVERS. Here's a book filled with great ideas that answer that frequent question, *"What should I do with these leftovers?"* This book is divided into convenient sections, giving recipes for leftover beef, pork, poultry, vegetables, etc. All recipes are family-taste-proven! With this book, you can serve a leftover dish and be asked, *"What's this new dish, Mom?"* Just $2.95.

FARM KITCHEN COOKERY. This cookbook contains some of the best country cooking you'll find anywhere, since the recipes come from *farm wives!* The book features winning recipes from 3 years of recipe contests, plus special chapters including field lunch menus. Just $2.95. Users of this book know what a bargain that is!

HOMEMADE BREADS. The rising popularity (pun intended) of baking bread at home is sweeping the country. With farm and ranch wives, it's long been a tradition. This recipe book includes a variety of recipes for white breads, whole wheat breads, rye breads, cheese breads, oatmeal breads, herb onion breads, raisin breads, yeast breads and other variety breads. Just $2.95.

To order any of these books or extra copies of "Pies Aplenty" at $2.95 per copy, simply name the book and send payment—along with 60¢ per order for postage and shipping—to: Country Store, P.O. Box 572, Milwaukee WI 53201.